CONTENTS

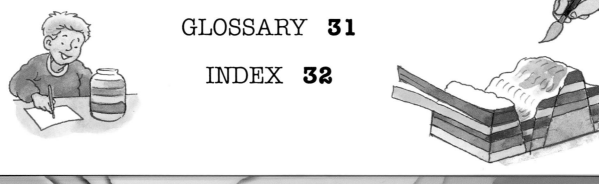

INTRODUCTION

Geography is about people and places and all the changes that take place in the world. How the shape of the land changes every time a glacier moves or a volcano erupts. How people make changes when they build roads and houses and chop down forests. Geography is about all these things. Learning about what's inside the Earth will help you understand why our world looks like it does and where our mountains came from.

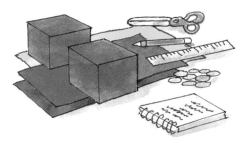

1 Look out for numbers like this. Each step for the projects inside the book has been numbered in this way. Make sure you follow the steps in the right order to find out how to make the projects.

MORE IDEAS
● Look out for the More Ideas boxes. They either give extra information about the project on the page, or they suggest other interesting things for you to make or do.

GEOGRAPHY *for fun*

Mountains

Moving

rth

obson

Franklin Watts
London • Sydney

This edition published in 2003
© Aladdin Books Ltd 2001

Produced by
Aladdin Books Ltd
28 Percy Street
London W1T 2BZ

First published in Great Britain
in 2001 by
Franklin Watts
96 Leonard Street
London EC2A 4XD

ISBN 0–7496–5352–3

Editor: Kathy Gemmell

Designer: Simon Morse

Illustrator: Tony Kenyon

Printed in UAE

A CIP catalogue record for this book
is available from the British Library.

The author, Pam Robson, is an experienced teacher.
She has written and advised on many books for children
on geography and science subjects.

WHAT'S HAPPENING

● The What's Happening paragraphs explain the geography behind the projects you do or make.

● Look out for Helpful Hints on some pages – they give you tips for doing the projects.

● Look up the Glossary at the back of the book to find out what important words mean.

WARNING

● This sign means that you must take care. Ask an adult to help you when you need to use a sharp knife or a hot liquid. When collecting information for projects, always tell an adult where you are going and what you are doing.

INSIDE THE EARTH

At the centre of the Earth is a hard inner core of metallic rock. It is surrounded by an outer core of hot liquid rock called magma. Next is a thick layer called the mantle, made up mainly of hard rock with some parts of magma. The magma causes rock in the Earth's thin top layer, called the crust, to move around.

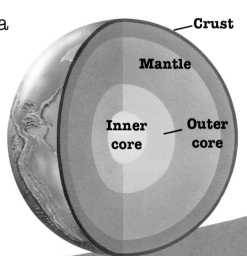

Crust

Mantle

Inner core

Outer core

CUT THROUGH THE WORLD

Make a colourful diagram, called a cross section, of the inside of the Earth. A cross section is like a 2D (two-dimensional) slice cut through Earth's core.

1 You will need four sheets of coloured paper and a large sheet of card. Use a compass to draw a dark-coloured circle with a radius of 12.5 cm, a red circle with a radius of 12 cm, an orange circle with a radius of 8 cm and a yellow circle with a radius of 4 cm. Cut out the circles.

Radius

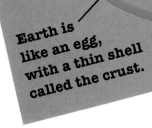

The inner core of hard rock is very hot.

Earth is like an egg, with a thin shell called the crust.

2 Glue the 12.5 cm circle onto the card. Line up all the centres of the circles. Now glue the 12 cm circle on top of the 12.5 cm circle. Glue the 8 cm circle on top of the 12 cm circle. Glue the 4 cm circle down last. Label each layer and decorate each one using pencils of the same colour.

The mantle, made up of hard rock and magma, is 3,000 km thick.

The outer core is made up of liquid magma.

GOING DOWN

● The deepest hole ever drilled into the Earth's crust is in Russia and is 13 km deep. This is about 4 km more than the height of Mount Everest, the world's highest mountain.

● The thickness of the Earth's crust varies. Beneath the oceans, it is around 6 km thick. Beneath continents, it can be 35 km thick. Beneath high mountains, the crust is even thicker.

Ocean

Continental crust

Oceanic crust

Mantle

MOVING PLATES

Earth's thin crust is made up of several pieces, called tectonic plates, which move around on top of magma in the mantle. When plates collide, mountain ranges form. When they slide past each other, there is an earthquake. When they separate or move beneath the mantle, a volcano erupts. Once, all the continents were joined in a huge landmass called Pangaea. Plate movement over millions of years caused them to drift to their present positions.

JIGSAW WORLD

Some of the continent shapes you see on maps can still be fitted together like a jigsaw to make part of Pangaea.

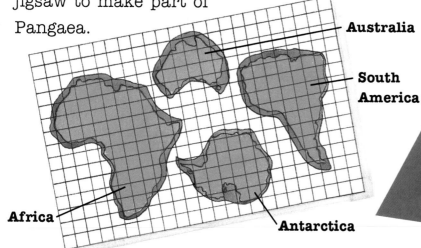

Australia

South America

Africa

Antarctica

1 Each shape above shows a continent or part of a continent. Count the squares in the orange part of each shape, then copy the outline onto squared paper with large squares. This will give you continents of the same shape, but bigger.

2 Now copy the blue outline around each of your enlarged continents. This represents the continental shelf – the part of the sea bed that the continent sits on. Continental shelves are the shallowest parts of the sea.

3 Glue the shapes onto a sheet of stiff card and colour them in. Make sure you colour the continental shelves blue. Then carefully cut out each shape.

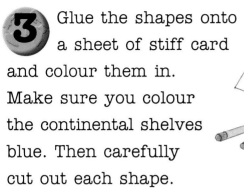

4 Piece together your jigsaw on a large tray. Look carefully at the red area on the big globe below to see what the finished jigsaw should look like.

Pangaea, 220 million years ago

COLLISION COURSE

● Some tectonic plates have drifted apart, but others have moved closer together. The subcontinent of India (in red below) was once further south. It gradually moved northwards until it collided with Asia. The mountains called the Himalayas were formed as the continental plates collided.

5 million years ago

135 million years ago

India

200 million years ago

● The plates that make up the oceanic crust also move. Here, beneath the sea, the rocks are much younger. As the plates pull apart, magma rises from the mantle and solidifies to form new rock.

SHAPING MOUNTAINS

Within the Earth's crust, there are layers of different rock. These layers are called strata. When moving tectonic plates collide, rock strata are forced upwards and shaped into mountains with sharp peaks. These are called fold mountains. The peaks of the Himalayas are fold mountains. So are the Andes, in South America, which are several ranges of mountains formed by plate movements.

FOLDING MOUNTAINS

To make a model showing how rock strata are pushed upwards to make high mountains, you will need some coloured plasticine and a knife.

1 Roll and shape plasticine into strips about 2 cm wide. Place the strips on top of each other and cut them to form a block of layers that look like rock strata.

2 Hold each end of your 'strata' block and gently push inwards. Watch the mountains fold. Make another block and repeat. See how many different mountain shapes you can make in this way.

WHAT'S HAPPENING

● The force of plates colliding makes rock strata at the plate edges buckle in different ways. Sometimes rock material from one plate is squeezed against the other plate. It crumples to form more mountains.

Fold mountains form as rock buckles under pressure.

Plate   **Plate**

CONE-SHAPED MOUNTAINS

Not all mountains are fold mountains. Many steep-sided mountains start as volcanoes. Over time, the lava cools and hardens into a cone shape (see page 14).

Layers of cooled lava

TRENCHES AND SEAMOUNTS

● Most oceans were formed after the break-up of Pangaea. The oceanic crust is still widening. As it collides with a continental plate, it slips below it and a trench forms. Many tectonic plate edges lie beneath the oceans. The Marianas Trench beneath the Pacific Ocean is the deepest trench in the world, over 10 km deep in places. Look it up in an atlas.

● As heat from inside the Earth rises, huge ridges push up underwater. These undersea mountains, called seamounts, are mostly cone-shaped.

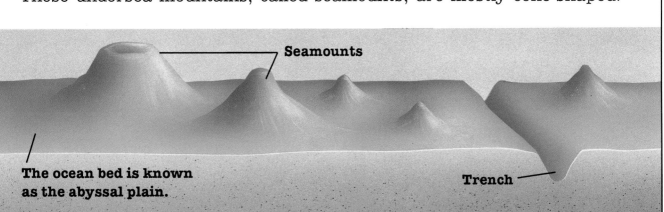

Seamounts

The ocean bed is known as the abyssal plain.

Trench

FAULTS AND EARTHQUAKES

As tectonic plates move around, rocks split and form cracks called faults. The land moves where there is a fault. Mountains with flat tops, called block mountains, form when the rock is forced up. Wide rift valleys form when the rock slips down between two faults. There is a large rift valley in East Africa. Earthquakes happen when rocks crack and move suddenly at a fault. In some parts of the world, such as Japan, this happens regularly.

BLOCK AND RIFT MODEL

To make this model, you will need a cardboard box, thin card, flour, cold water, newspaper, a craft knife, tape, glue, sand, paints and coloured paper.

1 Carefully copy the shape of the model shown here onto the sides of the box. Ask an adult to help you cut round the outline with a craft knife.

2 Cover the top of the box with the card. Use sticky tape to hold it in place.

3 Mix cold water and flour to make a paste. Crumple sheets of newspaper and dip them in the paste. Lay the crumpled newspaper on the model to give the land some shape.

4 When the model is dry, paint it with a mixture of sand and paint. This will give it a textured surface. Glue strips of coloured paper to the sides, as shown, to make strata.

WHAT'S HAPPENING

● Pressure pushing up from under the ground forces land upwards to create block mountains. A rift valley forms if the land between two parallel faults slips downwards.

Block mountain

Rift valley

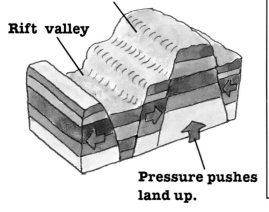

Pressure pushes land up.

EARTHQUAKES

● Earthquakes often happen at plate edges where two plates push against each other. Rocks can stand this pressure for many years, but eventually the strain becomes too great and the rocks snap into a new position. Vibrations caused by the sudden movement spread out from a point underground, called the focus, and make the ground shake.

Plates push against each other and stress builds.

The rocks snap into place, causing an earthquake.

Epicentre

Damage is worst at the epicentre, directly above the focus.

● The Richter scale measures energy released by an earthquake on a number scale from one to nine.

Small earthquake = up to 4.5

Moderate earthquake = 4.5 – 5.5

Major earthquake = 6.5 – 7.5

Great earthquake = more than 7.5

VOLCANOES

Volcanoes are mostly found on the edges of tectonic plates. They are vents or 'chimneys' in the Earth's crust, through which magma from the Earth's mantle erupts to the surface. On the surface, the magma cools to form lava. The lava flows in streams from the vents. Over thousands of years, the surfaces around the vents build up until mountains are formed. A volcano's shape depends on the kind of lava that erupts from it.

LOVELY LAVA

There are different kinds of lava, which flow at different speeds. Lava can be viscous (thick and sticky) like treacle, or very runny.

1 Use different lava-like liquids to find out which kind travels fastest down a slope. You will need a metal tray and some syrup, cooking oil and treacle.

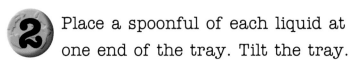

2 Place a spoonful of each liquid at one end of the tray. Tilt the tray. Use a watch that shows seconds to time how long each liquid takes to reach the bottom of the tray. Note down the times.

3 Now see how the times differ if you warm or cool the liquids. Ask an adult to help you put the containers in hot water for a while. Then repeat step 2, noting the new flow times. Now put the containers in cool water and repeat the project.

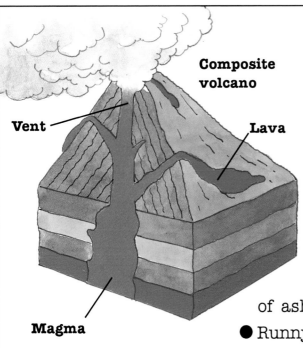

Composite volcano

Vent

Lava

Magma

VOLCANOES IN ACTION

● Viscous, cooler lava flows more slowly than hot, runny lava. Composite volcanoes have steep sides because they are formed by repeated and frequent flows of stiff, viscous lava. Volcanic eruptions from cones like these are extremely violent.

● Cinder volcanoes are also steep-sided, but are formed by layers of ash and cinder rather than lava.

● Runny lava erupts more gently, then spreads out. Shield and fissure volcanoes form in this way.

GEYSERS

● Underground water is sometimes heated by hot magma, and geysers of hot water shoot up out of the ground. These are used as sources of geothermal energy in countries like Iceland.

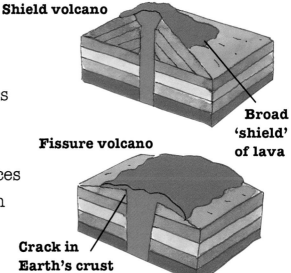

Shield volcano

Broad 'shield' of lava

Fissure volcano

Crack in Earth's crust

ROCKS AND MINERALS

The oldest rocks, called igneous rocks, contain crystals. Once igneous rocks have been broken down and changed by the weather, they become sedimentary, or second-hand, rocks. Layers of sedimentary rocks are called strata. Fossils are sometimes found in these rocks. Under certain conditions, sedimentary rock can change into another, harder kind of rock, called metamorphic rock.

**Granite
(igneous)**

**Sandstone
(sedimentary)**

**Marble
(metamorphic)**

SEDIMENT

To create your own sedimentary layers, you will need some gravel, sand and mud, a jar with a lid and some water.

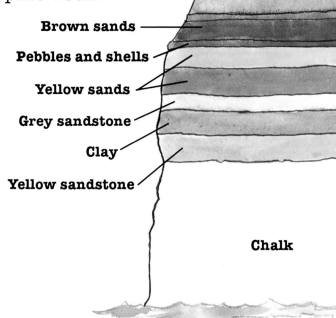

Soil and gr

Clay

Brown sands ——

Pebbles and shells ⁓

Yellow sands ⁓

Grey sandstone ⁓

Clay ⁓

Yellow sandstone ⁓

Chalk

1 Put equal amounts of sand, gravel and mud in layers inside the jar. Cover the layers with water.

● Igneous rocks, like granite, are being formed all the time inside the Earth. Sedimentary rocks, like sandstone, are worn-down igneous rocks. Immense heat and pressure can transform a sedimentary rock, like limestone, into a metamorphic rock, like marble.

2 Screw on the lid tightly, then shake the contents of the jar. Leave to settle for a few days. Layers of sediment will form.

3 Look closely at the layers. The material with the largest grains settles to the bottom of the jar. Smaller grained material comes to the top. Make drawings of your 'strata' and label them, as on the drawing opposite.

WHERE MINERALS COME FROM

● Rocks are made of minerals. Diamonds are minerals. They are the hardest material known, and are used to make cutting tools.

● A scale called Mohs' scale is used to grade the hardness of minerals. Diamonds are at the top of the scale at 10. Each mineral can cut the one below it on the scale. Topaz, at 8, is two places below diamond (see page 30).

Topaz

Diamond

● Magma from the Earth's core pushes up volcanic vents and solidifies under great heat and pressure. As it cools, crystals of pure carbon form inside the rock. These carbon crystals are diamonds. Slow cooling makes the largest crystals. As the rock breaks down, some diamond crystals come to the surface.

Some crystals are washed down to the sea.

Volcanic vent

MOUNTAINS AND MAPS

To design maps, cartographers (map-makers) need exact measurements of the land. Surveyors measure and calculate land height using an instrument called a theodolite. This means that maps can be drawn to scale and can show the exact shape of the land. Mountain heights are always measured from sea level.

MOUNTAIN MEASURE

To make and use a theodolite, you need a tape measure, a rectangle of stiff card, a small cardboard tube, thread, sticky tape, a ruler, a craft knife and string with a key attached.

1 Ask an adult to help you score the card diagonally using a ruler and craft knife. Cut it in half to make two right-angled triangles. Use only one half.

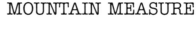

2 Cut the cardboard tube in half to make two viewers for your theodolite. To make 'sights', tape two pieces of crossed thread across the viewing end of each tube, as shown here.

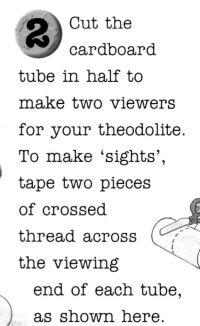

3 Tape a viewer to each end of the long side of the triangle. Make a hole at the top of the short side. Push the free end of the string with the key on it through the hole, then knot it so that the key hangs down. This is your plumb line.

HELPFUL HINTS

● Test your theodolite by trying it out on something you already know the height of. You may need to walk backwards or forwards until you can line up the viewers with the top of the object being measured.

4 Now look through the viewers and line up the centre of the sights with the top of a tree. Move forwards or backwards until the plumb line hangs straight down along the short side of the triangle.

(b)

(a)

5 Ask a friend to measure the distance between you and the foot of the tree (a). The height of the tree is that distance added to your own height (b).

SPOT HEIGHTS AND CONTOURS
Contours are lines on maps that join all places the same height above sea level. Where contours on a map are very close together, it means the land rises steeply. The highest point on a hill or mountain cannot be shown by contour lines. Instead, a spot height is written on the map showing the exact height at that point. Look in an atlas to find the exact height of Mount Everest.

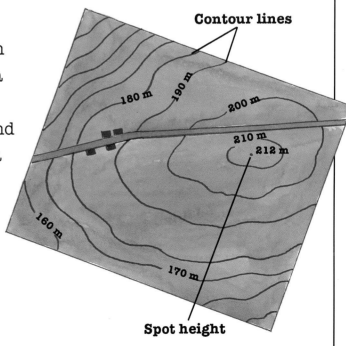

Contour lines

180 m

190 m

200 m

210 m

212 m

160 m

170 m

Spot height

HOW HIGH?

Altitude means height above sea level. At high altitudes, the air is thin because there is less oxygen in the Earth's atmosphere at that level. People born in high places have a large heart and lungs and wide nostrils to breathe more oxygen. The weight of air pressing down on Earth, called air pressure, is low at high altitudes. In the same way, water pressure is low near the surface (the top) of the sea.

Everest—8,848 m

Kilimanjaro—5,895 m

Ben Nevis—1,343 m

PRESSURE BOTTLE

Make a fountain to show water pressure at work. Air pressure works in the same way. You need an empty plastic bottle, a tray, a funnel, plasticine, paper, a compass, glue and coloured pencils.

1 Look in an atlas to find out the heights of three high mountains. Chart the heights on a picture graph, as shown. Glue the chart around the plastic bottle, leaving a gap down one side.

2 Use a compass to make three holes in the bottle. Position the holes vertically (one above the other) in the gap on the bottle. Make each hole level with the highest point of one of the mountains on your chart.

3 Before filling the plastic bottle with water, cover all three holes with plasticine. Make sure each hole is completely watertight.

4 Stand the bottle on a tray. Use a funnel to fill the bottle to the top with water. Carefully remove the three pieces of plasticine and watch what happens.

WHAT'S HAPPENING
● You will notice that the fountain of water at the top does not spurt as far as the two beneath. This is because water pressure is lower at the top than at the bottom. There is more water pushing down on the water at the bottom of the bottle than on the water at the top. In the same way, air pressure is lower at the top of a mountain than at the bottom.

CLEAR AIR
● Astronomers prefer to place telescopes at the tops of mountains because of the thinner, clearer air there. There are few clouds at high altitudes, which makes it much easier to see the stars and planets.

ICE AND SNOW

The higher you go, the colder the climate. Snow is found on mountain peaks, even close to the Equator. The level above which snow lies permanently is called the snow line. At the North Pole and South Pole, the snow line is at sea level. Ice forms beneath heavy snow, and rivers of ice called glaciers move slowly down mountain sides carving U-shaped valleys.

HOT WIRE

To show how ice can slide over rocky surfaces, like a glacier does, you will need an ice tray, a freezer, two supports, wire, a large tray and weights.

1 Fill a rectangular ice tray with water and freeze it. Remove your long ice cube from the dish and position it across the supports, like a bridge, on a large tray.

2 Ask an adult to help you make a wire sling to hold the weights, as shown. Loop a length of wire around the ice cube and attach its ends to the sling. The sling should hang straight down but not touch the tray.

3 Watch the wire as the heavy weights drag it slowly through the ice. The wire cuts through the ice, but the ice remains in one piece. Eventually, the wire will pass through the ice completely.

WHAT'S HAPPENING

● The pressure of the weighted wire melts the ice, letting the wire pass through it. But above the wire there is no pressure, so the ice freezes again. Below glaciers, the same thing happens as moving ice meets a large rock. The ice melts, flows around the rock and freezes again on the other side. Melting and re-freezing helps the ice slide over large obstacles.

Wire

MOVING ICE AND SNOW

● Glaciers can move round large rocks, but they pick up loose pieces of rock and carry them down mountain sides. These rocks wear away the ground beneath to form U-shaped valleys and also bowl-shaped hollows near mountain peaks, called corries or cirques.

● When heavy snow slides down a mountain side, it is called an avalanche. Avalanches often happen when the ground warms slightly and the first snowfall does not freeze hard. A loud noise, or skiers, can set off an avalanche. Whole villages can be buried under the snow.

The fjords in Norway were formed by glaciers.

U-shaped valley

Loose snow

RAIN SHADOW

Rain falls when warm, moist winds blow from the sea, reach land, then are forced to rise and cool over high mountain tops. Moisture in cooling air near mountain peaks condenses (turns into tiny droplets) to form clouds. When the clouds can hold no more moisture, rain falls. This is called orographic, or relief, rainfall. The far side of the mountain, called the lee side, remains dry, with no rainfall. It is said to be in the rain shadow of the mountain.

WHERE DID ALL THE RAIN GO?

Choose a very rainy day to observe the rain shadow beside a wall. You will need waterproof clothing, three containers (all the same shape and size) and a ruler.

Altitude increases

1 Wearing waterproofs, position one container right beside a wall, and the other two containers varying distances from it. As soon as the rain stops, bring the containers indoors. Be careful not to mix them up!

2 Measure the amount of water in each container. You should find that the container that was nearest the wall has the least water in it. The wall creates a rain shadow. Look at the ground near the wall. Does it seem drier than elsewhere?

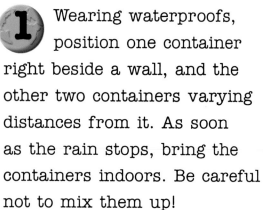

Pollution in the atmosphere

Acid rain

ACID RAIN

When it rains, gases in the air are dissolved. This makes all rainwater naturally slightly acidic. When rain falls on limestone rock, its natural acidity dissolves the rock. But pollution in the air can increase the amount of acidity in rainfall. This harmful acid rain can destroy trees (above), and eat away at stonework.

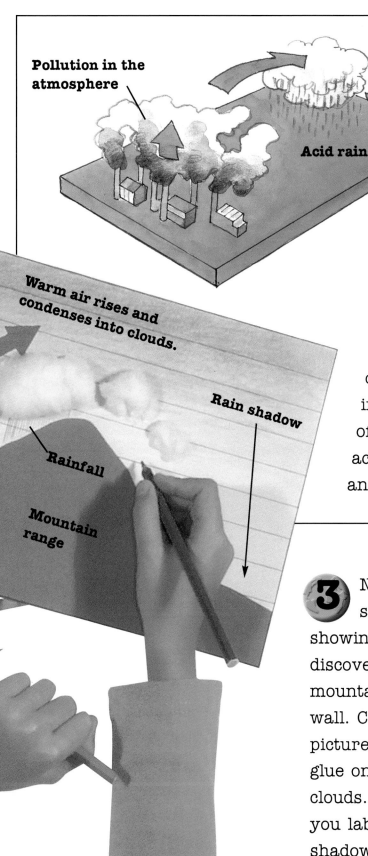

Warm air rises and condenses into clouds.

Rain shadow

Rainfall

Mountain range

3 Now make a rain shadow collage showing what you have discovered. Draw a mountain in place of the wall. Copy and colour the picture shown here then glue on cotton wool clouds. Make sure you label the rain shadow side of the mountain.

EROSION AND WEATHERING

Over time, land is worn away by rivers and seas, and also by weather. This is called erosion. The eroded material is carried away and left somewhere else. This is called deposition. Erosion and deposition always happen together. On mountain slopes, ice, wind, frost and rain wear away the rock. Water collects in cracks, freezes and causes the rock to break. Loose banks of stones may slide down slopes, forming screes.

CRACKING UP

Using balls of modelling clay rolled in cling film, you can carry out an experiment that shows why and how mountain rocks are eroded by frost and ice.

2 Freeze one of the balls of clay. Leave it in the freezer for 24 hours, then remove it. Allow it to thaw out completely then remove the cling film. What differences do you notice between the two balls of clay? Look at the cracks in the thawed clay.

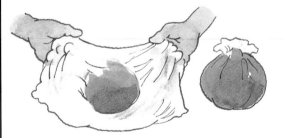

1 Roll two balls from damp modelling clay in the palm of your hands. Spray the outside of the clay with water. Then wrap each ball separately in cling film.

MUDSLIDES

● The clearing of trees from land is called deforestation. Mountain sides erode more quickly after people have chopped down trees. Soil on bare slopes is easily washed away by rain because tree roots no longer hold the soil in place. Heavy rain on eroded slopes can cause mudslides that destroy roads and bury whole villages.

WHAT'S HAPPENING

● Eventually, your frozen clay will shatter. The experiment has reproduced what happens, again and again, to rocks frozen by ice and frost on a mountain. Imagine rocks frozen many, many times over centuries. Eventually, those rocks crack and stones roll down the slopes to form screes.

● The clay shatters because ice fills more space than water, so ice in a crack pushes against the sides and opens the crack even further. Test this by filling a plastic bottle three-quarters full and freezing it. The ice will fill the bottle – or even break out of it!

3 Spray the thawed clay again. Cover it again with cling film and re-freeze. Remove after 24 hours and carry out another observation. Repeat this two or three times and note the changes each time.

TUNNELS AND PASSES

A long time ago, travelling across mountain ranges was dangerous and difficult. In remote places, it is still difficult. Road and rail tunnels now make it much easier for travellers to cross mountains. Designers and engineers must construct the strongest and safest structures for travellers. Tunnels do not spoil the countryside, but are expensive to build.

GOING THROUGH

To find out which tunnel shape is the strongest and safest, you will need coins or washers, glue, boxes or thick books, and thin card cut and folded into shapes.

1 Score, fold, roll and glue thin card into large 'tunnel' shapes, as shown. You need a cylinder (a), a cuboid (b), a prism (c) and an arch shape (d).

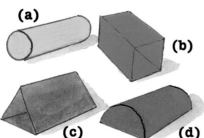

(a)
(b)
(c)
(d)

2 Make a bridge by placing two boxes or piles of books about 15 cm apart and laying thin card 30 cm long between them. Make sure your 'tunnel' shapes support the bridge in the middle. Lower the supports if necessary.

4 Compare exactly how many coins are added to the bridge for each shape and record your results on a chart. The round and arched shapes should hold the most coins.

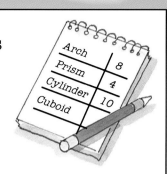

Arch	8
Prism	4
Cylinder	10
Cuboid	

WHAT'S HAPPENING

● No corners in a shape mean extra strength. Edges and corners are weak points. The bridge above the round and arched tunnels held firm the longest because the weight was spread over the whole tunnel roof.

3 Position a 'tunnel' beneath the bridge. Add coins to the top of the bridge. Note how many coins are needed until the tunnel begins to bend out of shape. Repeat this for every shape.

MOUNTAIN PASSES

● Places that cut through mountain ranges, where people can cross, are called passes. They are deep valleys that have been eroded by glaciers which were unable to join the main glacier moving down a slope. Roads built through passes often have dangerous hairpin bends because the sides of the pass are so steep.

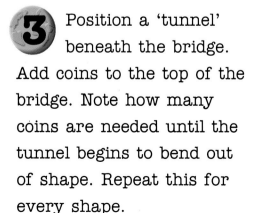

HIGHEST, LONGEST AND LARGEST

A mountain is an area of high land, higher and steeper than a hill. As you go up a mountain, the temperature falls 2 degrees Celsius for every 300 m you climb.

Some of the world's highest mountains

Mt Everest, Nepal – 8,848 m

Mt Aconcagua, Argentina – 6,960 m

Mt McKinley, Alaska – 6,194 m

Mt Kilimanjaro, Tanzania – 5,895 m

Mt Elbrus, Russian Federation – 5,642 m

The tallest volcanic peak is Mauna Kea, Hawaii. From its base below the sea to its peak, it is 10,203 m high.

The highest volcano on land is Aconcagua in the Andes Mountains, Argentina. It is 6,960 m high, but is now extinct (has stopped erupting).

The tallest active volcano on land is Ojos del Salado, between Chile and Argentina. It is 6,887 m high.

The tallest active geyser is Steamboat Geyser in Yellowstone National Park, Wyoming, USA. Plumes 100 m high rise every few weeks.

The largest earthquakes ever recorded – measuring 8.6 on the Richter scale – were at Gansu, China in 1920 (170,000 people died) and Valparaiso, Chile in 1906 (20,000 people died).

The biggest volcanic eruption of recent times was Tambora, Indonesia in 1815. It left an 11 km crater and killed 90,000 people.

The coldest place on Earth is Vostock Station in Antarctica, where a temperature of –89 degrees Celsius has been recorded.

The longest glacier in the world is the Lambert glacier in Antarctica, which is about 400 km long.

The longest mountain railway tunnel is the Simplon tunnel through the Alps. It is nearly 20 km long.

The longest mountain road tunnel is the St Gothard road tunnel in Switzerland. It is over 16 km long.

Tectonic plates move between 2 and 20 cm each year.

Mohs' scale of mineral hardness: 1 Talc; 2 Gypsum; 3 Calcite; 4 Fluorite; 5 Apatite; 6 Feldspar; 7 Quartz; 8 Topaz; 9 Corundum; 10 Diamond.

GLOSSARY

Acid rain
Rainfall that contains too much acid, caused by pollution.

Cirques (or **corries**)
Bowl-shaped hollows on mountain slopes, shaped by glaciers and often containing lakes.

Climate
The average weather in a place over the year.

Continental shelf
The part of the sea bed that a continent sits on.

Core
The metallic centre of the Earth.

Crust
The Earth's hard outer shell.

Crystals
Solids with particles arranged in a regular order, forming flat sides or faces.

Fjords
Long, narrow inlets of sea between steep cliffs shaped by glaciers. Common in Norway.

Fossils
Evidence of ancient life found in sedimentary rocks.

Geothermal energy
Natural heat from inside the Earth.

Geysers
Hot springs that throw up columns of heated water at intervals.

Igneous rocks
Rocks formed when either magma or cooled lava solidifies.

Magma
Hot molten (liquid) rock formed deep inside the Earth. Called lava when it erupts on the surface.

Mantle
The part of the interior of the Earth that lies between the core and the crust.

Metamorphic rocks
Igneous or sedimentary rocks that have been changed due to great heat and pressure inside the Earth.

Minerals
What rocks are made of. Most have particles arranged in a regular order, forming crystals.

Mohs' scale
Used to measure the hardness of minerals.

Richter scale
Used to measure the strength of earthquakes.

Sedimentary rocks
Rocks formed from sediment, which is matter carried by water or wind and deposited on the land.

Strata
Layers of sedimentary rocks.

Subcontinents
Large landmasses smaller than continents, like India.

Tectonic plates
Large blocks of the Earth's crust that float on the liquid magma beneath.

INDEX

PICTURE CREDITS
Abbreviations: t-top, m-middle, b-bottom, r-right, l-left, c-centre.
All photographs supplied by Select Pictures, except for:
5tl, 14m - Digital Stock; 11tl - Mark Newman/FLPA; 23mr - Bill
Broadhurst/FLPA; 25tr, 27tl - Silvestris Fotoservice/FLPA;
26tl - Derek Hall/FLPA. 28m - David Hosking/FLPA.